MAIN
DISCARD
SEP 2 0 2012

D1318896

TRADITIONAL FAMILY CAKES

TRADITIONAL FAMILY CAKES

OLDHAM COUNTY PUBLIC LIBRARY
308 YAGER AVENUE
LAGRANGE, KY 40031

This edition published in 2011

LOVE FOOD is an imprint of Parragon Books Ltd

Parragon
Queen Street House
4 Queen Street
Bath BA1 1HE, UK

Copyright © Parragon Books Ltd 2011

LOVE FOOD and the accompanying heart device is a registered trademark of Parragon Books Ltd in Australia, the UK, USA, India, and the EU.

All rights reserved. No part of this publication may be reproduced, stored in a retrieval system, or transmitted, in any form or by any means, electronic, mechanical, photocopying, recording, or otherwise, without the prior permission of the copyright holder.

ISBN: 978-1-4454-2297-8

Printed in Indonesia

Cover and new photography by Clive Streeter
Home economy and new recipes by Angela Drake

Notes for the reader
This book uses imperial, metric, and US cup measurements. Follow the same units of measurement throughout; do not mix imperial and metric. All spoon measurements are level: teaspoons are assumed to be 5 ml, and tablespoons are assumed to be 15 ml. Unless otherwise stated, milk is assumed to be whole, individual vegetables, such as potatoes, are medium, eggs are large, and pepper is freshly ground black pepper.

The times given are an approximate guide only. Preparation times differ according to the techniques used by different people and the cooking times may also vary from those given as a result of the type of oven used. Optional ingredients, variations or serving suggestions have not been included in the calculations.

Recipes using raw or very lightly cooked eggs should be avoided by infants, the elderly, pregnant women, convalescents, and anyone with a chronic condition. Pregnant and breastfeeding women are advised to avoid eating peanuts and peanut products. People with nut allergies should be aware that some of the ready-prepared ingredients used in the recipes in this book may contain nuts. Always check the packaging before use.

Contents

Introduction

From a simple Cherry Cake to a moist and sticky iced Gingerbread Cake, luscious Lemon Cake, or an indulgent Chocolate Fudge Cake, nothing can beat the flavor of a homemade cake. The wonderful aroma that fills the air from a warm kitchen and the satisfaction of presenting your own creation to family or friends is so rewarding that it's no wonder that home baking is as popular now as it ever was.

This book contains a collection of traditional cake recipes that are easy to make with clear instructions and simple frostings and decorations. Whether it's a coffee break, afternoon get-together with friends, birthday treat, or a special celebration, you'll find a cake to fit the occasion.

The Basic Ingredients

As with any type of cooking, it's worth buying good-quality basic ingredients. For the best flavor, choose a lightly salted or unsalted butter. Soft margarine can be used instead of butter, but avoid low-fat spreads because they have a high water content and an inferior taste.

Always use the correct size egg. Unless specified, all the recipes in this book use large eggs. Let the eggs come to room temperature for about 1 hour before using.

Check that flours and leavening agents are not past their expiration date. Stale flour will impart an unpleasant taste and leavening agents can lose their effectiveness, resulting in a heavy textured cake.

Superfine sugar is the best sugar for cake making—its fine grains dissolve easily when creamed with butter. If you don't have superfine sugar, process the same amount of granulated sugar in a food processor for 1 minute. To make your own vanilla sugar, simply put a vanilla bean into a container of superfine sugar and leave for 5–6 days. Chocolate and darker fruitcakes are often made with brown sugars because they add a richer color and flavor.

Essential Equipment

Any reasonably equipped kitchen should have most of the basics needed for making cakes—bowls, spoons, spatulas, a sifter, and a wire rack for cooling. A good set of measuring cups and spoons to guarantee accuracy is also essential and an electric handheld mixer will make light work of beating and whisking.

The only other major items to buy are the appropriate size cake pans. You'll need a range of shapes and sizes, so you'll probably have to build up your collection gradually. When buying, pick sturdy cake pans that will last—flimsy pans may buckle quickly and have to be replaced. If you buy pans with a nonstick coating, take care not to scratch the lining with metal utensils. Always wash pans thoroughly after use and place in a warm oven to dry out completely before putting them away. An alternative to metal pans is to try flexible nonstick silicone bakeware—you'll find a good range of shapes, sizes, and colors, and they are easy to use and clean.

Secrets of Success

Always read the recipe before you start baking. Make sure that you have all the ingredients at hand (at room temperature, if necessary). Measure the ingredients accurately—this is especially important with leavening agents, such as baking powder or baking soda, because too much or too little can have a drastic effect on the finished cake.

Before turning on the oven, make sure the shelves are in the correct position. Plan for at least 10 minutes for the oven to preheat to the required temperature. If you have a convection oven, check the manufacturers' instructions—you may need to reduce the temperature. Once the cake is in the oven, don't open the door too soon or too often because the cold air will lower the temperature and the cake may sink.

Use a cake pan that is the correct size, and take time to prepare it. Lightly grease with melted butter or a flavorless cooking oil, then line with parchment paper, cutting it to fit neatly.

There are two ways to test whether a cake is cooked. For a light yellow cake, simply press the top of the cake gently with your fingertips. The cake should feel springy to the touch and give very lightly, leaving no imprint. For richer cakes or fruitcakes, it's best to insert a toothpick into the center of the cake, then pull it out quickly—the toothpick should come away clean. If there is any cake batter on the toothpick, return the cake to the oven and bake for a little longer.

Freshly baked cakes are very fragile, so let them cool in the pan for 5–15 minutes before turning them out. Run a thin spatula around the edge of the pan to loosen the cake before inverting onto a wire rack. To prevent marks on the top of delicate yellow cakes, quickly flip them onto another rack. Let rich fruitcakes cool completely in the pan before turning out.

Common Cake Dilemmas

- If the cake has sunk in the middle—has too much leavening agent been used, the oven door been opened too soon, or the cake not been cooked for long enough?
- If the cake has a dry and crumbly texture—has the cake been cooked for too long or has too much baking powder been used?
- If the dried fruit sinks to the bottom of cake—is the cake batter too slack or the oven temperature too low?
- If the cake has not risen—has too little leavening agent been used or has the cake batter been overbeaten?
- Always make sure the cake is completely cold before storing it in an airtight container. If the cake is still a little warm, condensation may form, which can cause mold to grow on the surface.
- If the cake has a fresh cream or soft cheese filling or frosting, it will need to be stored in the refrigerator, but let it stand at room temperature for about 30 minutes before serving.
- Some cakes, such as gingerbread, will improve in flavor if kept for a few days before serving. Wrap well in wax paper and then aluminum foil to prevent them from drying out.
- Many cakes freeze well. Place in large freezer bags or wrap in aluminum foil, excluding as much air as possible. Unwrap and let stand at room temperature to thaw thoroughly.

CLASSIC CAKES

1

Chocolate Fudge Cake

SERVES 8

◆ Cooking time:
30–35 minutes

INGREDIENTS
✳ ¾ cup butter, softened,
plus extra for greasing
✳ heaping 1 cup superfine
sugar
✳ 3 eggs, beaten
✳ 3 tbsp light corn syrup
✳ 3 tbsp ground almonds
✳ heaping 1 cup
self-rising flour
✳ pinch of salt
✳ ¼ cup unsweetened
cocoa

FROSTING
✳ 8 oz/225 g semisweet
chocolate, broken into
pieces
✳ ¼ cup dark brown sugar
✳ 1 cup butter, diced
✳ 5 tbsp evaporated milk
✳ ½ tsp vanilla extract

Everyone loves a good chocolate cake and this moist chocolate cake smothered in a rich fudge frosting is one of the best! It is ideal for serving at a special celebration or as a delicious chocolate dessert.

1. Grease and line two 8-inch/20-cm round layer cake pans.

2. To make the frosting, place the chocolate, brown sugar, butter, evaporated milk, and vanilla extract in a heavy-bottom pan. Heat gently, stirring continuously, until melted. Pour into a bowl and let cool. Cover and let chill in the refrigerator for 1 hour, or until spreadable.

3. Preheat the oven to 350°F/180°C. Place the butter and superfine sugar in a bowl and beat together until light and fluffy. Gradually beat in the eggs. Stir in the corn syrup and ground almonds. Sift the flour, salt, and cocoa into a separate bowl, then fold into the cake batter. Add a little water, if necessary, to make a dropping consistency.

4. Spoon the cake batter into the prepared pans and bake in the preheated oven for 30–35 minutes, or until springy to the touch and a toothpick inserted in the center comes out clean.

5. Let stand in the pans for 5 minutes, then turn out onto wire racks to cool completely. When the cakes have cooled, sandwich them together with half of the frosting. Spread the remaining frosting over the top and sides of the cake, swirling it to give a frosted appearance.

HELPFUL HINT
Use a small palette knife to swirl the frosting evenly over the top and sides of the cake.

Lemon Cake

SERVES 8

◆ Cooking time:
45–60 minutes

INGREDIENTS

✱ butter, for greasing

✱ 1¾ cups all-purpose flour

✱ 2 tsp baking powder

✱ 1 cup superfine sugar

✱ 4 eggs

✱ ⅔ cup sour cream

✱ grated rind of 1 large lemon

✱ 4 tbsp lemon juice

✱ ⅔ cup sunflower oil

SYRUP

✱ 4 tbsp confectioners' sugar

✱ 3 tbsp lemon juice

This cake has a tangy lemon sugar syrup drizzled over it while still warm, which permeates through the cake to give it a wonderful moistness and extra lemony flavor.

1. Preheat the oven to 350°F/180°C. Grease and line an 8-inch/20-cm loose-bottom round cake pan.

2. Sift the flour and baking powder into a mixing bowl and stir in the superfine sugar.

3. In a separate bowl, whisk the eggs, sour cream, lemon rind, lemon juice, and oil together.

4. Pour the egg mixture into the dry ingredients and mix well until evenly combined.

5. Pour the batter into the prepared pan and bake in the preheated oven for 45–60 minutes, or until risen and golden brown.

6. Meanwhile, to make the syrup, mix together the confectioners' sugar and lemon juice in a small saucepan. Stir over low heat until just beginning to bubble and turn syrupy.

7. As soon as the cake comes out of the oven, prick the surface all over with a fine toothpick, then brush the syrup over the top. Let the cake cool completely in the pan before turning out and serving.

HELPFUL HINT

For a crunchy lemon crust, make the lemon syrup with granulated sugar instead of confectioners' sugar.

Carrot Cake

SERVES 10

◆ Cooking time:
1 hour–1 hour 10 minutes

INGREDIENTS

✳ oil or melted butter,
for greasing
✳ 1½ cups all-purpose
flour
✳ 1 tbsp baking powder
✳ 1 tsp ground cinnamon
✳ ½ tsp ground ginger
✳ ¾ cup unsalted butter,
softened
✳ heaping ¾ cup light
brown sugar
✳ 3 eggs, beaten
✳ 2 tbsp orange juice
✳ scant 1½ cups coarsely
grated carrots
✳ ½ cup chopped pecans
✳ pecan halves,
to decorate

FROSTING

✳ ¼ cup cream cheese
✳ 2¼ cups confectioners'
sugar
✳ finely grated rind of
1 orange
✳ 1 tbsp orange juice,
plus extra if needed

Sometimes called Passion Cake, this classic afternoon treat is made with grated carrots that soften during baking to give a deliciously moist texture and sweet flavor. Once frosted, this cake is best kept in the refrigerator, but let stand at room temperature for at least 30 minutes before serving.

1. Preheat the oven to 325°F/160°C. Grease and line a 9-inch/23-cm round cake pan.

2. Sift the flour, baking powder, cinnamon, and ginger into a bowl and add the butter, sugar, and eggs. Beat well until smooth, then stir in the orange juice, carrots, and chopped pecans.

3. Spoon the batter into the prepared pan and smooth the surface. Bake in the preheated oven for 1 hour–1 hour 10 minutes, or until well risen, firm, and golden brown.

4. Let cool in the pan for 10 minutes, then turn out onto a wire rack to finish cooling.

5. For the frosting, put all the ingredients into a bowl and beat until smooth and thick, adding more orange juice, if necessary. Spread over the top of the cake and decorate with pecan halves.

HELPFUL HINT
Instead of the pecans, decorate with tiny carrots shaped from orange-colored marzipan or fondant icing.

Coffee & Walnut Cake

SERVES 8

✦ Cooking time:
20–25 minutes

INGREDIENTS

✳ ¾ cup butter, plus extra
for greasing

✳ ¾ cup light brown
sugar

✳ 3 extra large eggs,
beaten

✳ 3 tbsp strong black
coffee

✳ 1½ cups self-rising
flour

✳ 1½ tsp baking powder

✳ 1 cup walnut pieces

✳ walnut halves,
to decorate

FROSTING

✳ ½ cup butter

✳ 1¾ cups confectioners'
sugar

✳ 1 tbsp strong black
coffee

✳ ½ tsp vanilla extract

Coffee and walnuts complement each other perfectly in this much loved layer cake. The layers are packed with chopped walnuts and the creamy coffee frosting has just the right touch of sweetness.

1. Preheat the oven to 350°F/180°C. Grease and line two 8-inch/20-cm round layer cake pans.

2. Beat the butter and brown sugar together until pale and fluffy. Gradually add the eggs, beating well after each addition. Beat in the coffee.

3. Sift the flour and baking powder into the mixture, then fold in lightly and evenly with a metal spoon. Fold in the walnut pieces.

4. Divide the batter between the prepared cake pans and smooth the surfaces. Bake in the preheated oven for 20–25 minutes, or until golden brown and springy to the touch. Turn out onto a wire rack to cool.

5. For the frosting, beat together the butter, confectioners' sugar, coffee, and vanilla extract, mixing until smooth and creamy.

6. Use about half of the frosting to sandwich the cakes together, then spread the remaining frosting on top and swirl with a metal spatula. Decorate with walnut halves.

HELPFUL HINT
For the best flavor, use a strong espresso coffee or a good-quality, strong instant coffee powder.

Iced Pound Loaf

SERVES 8–10

◆ Cooking time:
1–1¼ hours

INGREDIENTS

✳ ¾ cup unsalted butter, softened, plus extra for greasing
✳ heaping ¾ cup superfine sugar
✳ finely grated rind of 1 lemon
✳ 3 eggs, lightly beaten
✳ 1¼ cups self-rising flour
✳ 1 cup all-purpose flour
✳ 2 tbsp milk
✳ 1 tbsp lemon juice

ICING

✳ 1½ cups confectioners' sugar
✳ 2–3 tbsp lemon juice
✳ 2 tsp lemon curd, warmed

This classic cake has a fairly firm texture with a buttery flavor. Topped with a tangy lemon icing, it makes the perfect afternoon treat.

1. Preheat the oven to 325°F/160°C. Grease and line a 9 x 5 x 3-inch/23 x 13 x 8-cm loaf pan.

2. Place the butter and superfine sugar in a large bowl and beat together until very pale and fluffy. Beat in the lemon rind, then gradually beat in the eggs.

3. Sift the self-rising and all-purpose flours into the mixture and fold in gently until thoroughly incorporated. Fold in the milk and lemon juice.

4. Spoon the cake batter into the prepared pan and bake in the preheated oven for 1–1¼ hours, or until well risen, golden brown, and a toothpick inserted into the center comes out clean. Cool in the pan for 15 minutes, then turn out onto a wire rack to cool completely.

5. For the icing, sift the confectioners' sugar into a bowl. Add the lemon juice and stir to make a smooth and thick icing. Gently spread the icing over the top of the cake. Drizzle the warmed lemon curd over the top and drag a toothpick through the icing to create a swirled effect. Let set.

HELPFUL HINT

Cover the top of the cake loosely with aluminum foil after about 50 minutes to prevent overbrowning.

2

4

5

Classic Cherry Cake

SERVES 8

◆ Cooking time: 1–1¼ hours

INGREDIENTS

* heaping 1 cup candied cherries, quartered
* ¾ cup ground almonds
* 1¾ cups all-purpose flour
* 1 tsp baking powder
* scant 1 cup butter, plus extra for greasing
* 1 cup superfine sugar
* 3 extra large eggs
* finely grated rind and juice of 1 lemon
* 6 sugar cubes, crushed

This traditional favorite is dotted with sweet, red candied cherries, flavored with lemon rind and juice, and topped with crushed sugar cubes. To stop the cherries from sinking to the bottom during baking, the trick is to wash and dry them thoroughly before using to remove sticky glaze.

1. Preheat the oven to 350°F/180°C. Grease and line an 8-inch/20-cm round cake pan.

2. Stir together the candied cherries, ground almonds, and 1 tablespoon of the flour. Sift the remaining flour into a separate bowl with the baking powder.

3. Beat the butter and sugar together until light in color and fluffy in texture. Gradually add the eggs, beating hard with each addition, until evenly mixed.

4. Add the flour mixture and fold lightly and evenly into the creamed mixture with a metal spoon. Add the cherry mixture and fold in evenly. Finally, fold in the lemon rind and juice.

5. Spoon the batter into the prepared cake pan and sprinkle with the crushed sugar cubes. Bake in the preheated oven for 1–1¼ hours, or until risen, golden brown, and the cake is just beginning to shrink away from the sides of the pan.

6. Cool in the pan for about 15 minutes, then turn out to finish cooling on a wire rack.

HELPFUL HINT

If the batter starts to curdle when beating in the eggs, add a spoonful of the flour.

Banana Loaf

◆ Cooking time:
1 hour

INGREDIENTS

✳ butter, for greasing

✳ scant 1 cup self-rising flour

✳ scant ¾ cup whole wheat flour

✳ heaping ¾ cup raw brown sugar

✳ 1 tsp baking powder

✳ ¼ tsp salt

✳ ½ tsp ground cinnamon

✳ ½ tsp ground nutmeg

✳ 2 large ripe bananas, peeled

✳ ¾ cup orange juice

✳ 2 eggs, beaten

✳ 4 tbsp canola oil

The banana loaf has been a staple of baking cookbooks since the 1930s. This tasty loaf is a great way to use up overripe bananas so often left in the fruit bowl. It has a lovely, moist texture and will keep well for 3–4 days. The simplicity of the recipe means that it is popular with novice bakers.

1. Preheat the oven to 350°F/180°C. Grease and line a 9 x 5 x 3-inch/23 x 13 x 8-cm loaf pan.

2. Sift the flours, sugar, baking powder, salt, and the spices into a large bowl. In a separate bowl, mash the bananas with the orange juice, then stir in the eggs and oil. Pour into the dry ingredients and mix well.

3. Spoon the batter into the prepared loaf pan and bake in the preheated oven for 1 hour, then test to see if the loaf is cooked by inserting a toothpick into the center. If it comes out clean, the loaf is done. If not, bake for an additional 10 minutes and test again.

4. Remove from the oven and let cool in the pan. Turn out the loaf, slice, and serve.

HELPFUL HINT
Add a handful of raisins for an extra fruity flavor or some finely chopped pecans.

Gingerbread Cake

SERVES 12

✦ Cooking time:
1–1¼ hours

INGREDIENTS

✳ 2¼ cups all-purpose flour
✳ 1 tsp baking soda
✳ 1½ tsp ground ginger
✳ 1 tsp apple pie spice
✳ ½ cup butter, plus extra for greasing
✳ heaping ½ cup dark brown sugar
✳ scant ¾ cup light corn syrup
✳ scant ¼ cup molasses
✳ 2 extra large eggs, beaten
✳ 2 tbsp milk

ICING

✳ 1 cup confectioners' sugar
✳ 1 tbsp preserved ginger syrup
✳ 1–2 tbsp water
✳ 1 piece preserved ginger, finely chopped

The flavor of this cake will improve with time. If you have the patience, wrap the unfrosted cake in wax paper and store in a cool place for a few days before icing.

1. Preheat the oven to 325°F/160°C. Grease and line a 7-inch/18-cm square cake pan.

2. Sift the flour, baking soda, ground ginger, and apple pie spice into a large bowl. Place the butter, sugar, light corn syrup, and molasses in a pan and heat gently, stirring continuously, until the butter has melted. Cool for 5 minutes.

3. Stir the melted mixture into the bowl and mix well. Add the eggs and milk and beat until thoroughly incorporated.

4. Spoon the cake batter into the prepared pan and bake in the preheated oven for 1–1¼ hours, or until well risen and firm to the touch. Cool in the pan for 15 minutes, then turn out onto a wire rack to cool completely.

5. For the icing, sift the confectioners' sugar into a bowl. Stir in the preserved ginger syrup and enough of the water to make a smooth icing that just coats the back of a wooden spoon.

6. Spoon the icing over the top of the cake, letting it run down the sides. Sprinkle the preserved ginger over it and let set.

HELPFUL HINT
For a fruity flavor,
top the gingerbread batter with
thin slices of apple before baking.

2

4

6

Fruity Layer Cake

SERVES 8

◆ Cooking time:
25–30 minutes

INGREDIENTS

✳ 1¼ cups self-rising flour
✳ 1 tsp baking powder
✳ ¾ cup butter, softened, plus extra for greasing
✳ scant 1 cup superfine sugar
✳ 3 eggs
✳ confectioners' sugar, for dusting

FILLING

✳ 3 tbsp raspberry jelly
✳ 1¼ cups heavy cream, whipped
✳ 16 fresh strawberries, halved

This classic layer cake is given the star treatment with a luxurious filling of jelly, softly whipped cream, and fresh strawberries. Just perfect for a summer afternoon treat.

1. Preheat the oven to 350°F/180°C, then grease and line two 8-inch/20-cm round layer cake pans.

2. Sift the flour and baking powder into a bowl and add the butter, superfine sugar, and eggs. Mix together, then beat well until smooth.

3. Divide the batter evenly between the prepared pans and smooth the surfaces. Bake in the preheated oven for 25–30 minutes, or until well risen, golden brown, and the cakes feel springy when lightly pressed.

4. Let cool in the pans for 5 minutes, then turn out and peel off the lining paper. Transfer to wire racks to cool completely. Join the cakes together with the raspberry jelly, whipped heavy cream, and strawberry halves. Dust with confectioners' sugar and serve.

HELPFUL HINT

To create a lacy pattern on the cake, place a decorative paper napkin over the cake, dust with confectioners' sugar, then lift the paper off.

Date & Walnut Loaf

SERVES 8

◆ Cooking time:
35–40 minutes

INGREDIENTS

✴ heaping ½ cup chopped pitted dates
✴ ½ tsp baking soda
✴ finely grated rind of ½ lemon
✴ scant ½ cup hot tea
✴ 3 tbsp butter, plus extra for greasing
✴ ⅓ cup light brown sugar
✴ 1 egg
✴ heaping 1 cup self-rising flour
✴ ¼ cup chopped walnuts
✴ walnut halves, to decorate

Dried dates soaked in hot tea until softened give this loaf a lovely moist and crumbly texture. It is delicious when lightly spread with unsalted butter.

1. Preheat the oven to 350°F/180°C. Grease and line a 9 x 5 x 3-inch/23 x 13 x 8-cm loaf pan.

2. Place the dates, baking soda, and lemon rind in a bowl and add the hot tea. Let soak for 10 minutes, until the dates are softened.

3. Beat the butter and sugar together until light and fluffy, then beat in the egg. Stir the date mixture into this butter mixture.

4. Fold in the flour, using a large metal spoon, then fold in the chopped walnuts. Spoon the batter into the prepared loaf pan and smooth the surface. Top with the walnut halves.

5. Bake in the preheated oven for 35–40 minutes, or until risen, firm, and golden brown. Cool for 10 minutes in the pan, then turn out onto a wire rack to cool completely.

HELPFUL HINT
Choose a fragrant tea for soaking the dates, such as Earl Grey, or use a good-quality English Breakfast Tea.

FRUIT & NUT CAKES

2

Rich Fruitcake

SERVES 16

✦ Cooking time:
2¼–2¾ hours

INGREDIENTS

✳ scant 2½ cups golden raisins

✳ 1⅔ cups raisins

✳ ½ cup chopped plumped dried apricots

✳ ½ cup chopped pitted dates

✳ 4 tbsp dark rum or brandy, plus extra for flavoring (optional)

✳ finely grated rind and juice of 1 orange

✳ 1 cup butter, plus extra for greasing

✳ 1 cup light brown sugar

✳ 4 eggs

✳ heaping ⅓ cup chopped candied peel

✳ ⅓ cup candied cherries, quartered

✳ 2 tbsp chopped candied ginger or preserved ginger

✳ ⅓ cup chopped blanched almonds

✳ 1¾ cups all-purpose flour

✳ 1 tsp apple pie spice

A good choice of cake for celebrations, such as weddings and Christmas, this classic favorite should be made well in advance so there is time for the rich flavors to mature.

1. Place the golden raisins, raisins, apricots, and dates in a large bowl and stir in the rum, orange rind, and orange juice. Cover and let soak for several hours or overnight.

2. Preheat the oven to 300°F/150°C. Grease and line an 8-inch/20-cm round deep cake pan.

3. Beat the butter and sugar together until light and fluffy. Gradually beat in the eggs, beating hard after each addition. Stir in the soaked fruits, candied peel, candied cherries, candied ginger, and blanched almonds.

4. Sift the flour and apple pie spice, then fold lightly and evenly into the mixture. Spoon into the prepared cake pan and smooth the surface, making a slight depression in the center with the back of the spoon.

5. Bake in the preheated oven for 2¼–2¾ hours, or until the cake is beginning to shrink away from the sides of the pan and a toothpick inserted into the center comes out clean. Cool completely in the pan.

6. Turn out the cake and remove the lining paper. Wrap with wax paper and foil and store for at least 2 months before use. To add a richer flavor, prick the cake with a toothpick and spoon over a couple of tablespoons of rum or brandy, if using, before storing.

HELPFUL HINT
Make sure to wrap the cake well before storing. Keep in a dry, cool place.

Orange Bundt Cake

SERVES 10

✦ Cooking time:
45–50 minutes

INGREDIENTS

✳ scant 1 cup unsalted butter, plus extra for greasing

✳ 1 cup superfine sugar

✳ 3 extra large eggs, beaten

✳ finely grated rind of 1 orange

✳ ¼ cup poppy seeds

✳ 2¼ cups all-purpose flour, plus extra for dusting

✳ 2 tsp baking powder

✳ ⅔ cup milk

✳ ½ cup orange juice

✳ strips of orange zest, to decorate

SYRUP

✳ scant ¾ cup superfine sugar

✳ ⅔ cup orange juice

Bundt cakes are named after the distinctive fluted tube pans they are baked in. This version is a lovely soft yellow cake full of poppy seeds and soaked in a sweet orange syrup.

1. Preheat the oven to 325°F/160°C. Grease and lightly flour a Bundt ring pan, about 9½ inches/24 cm in diameter and with a capacity of approximately 8¾ cups.

2. Beat the butter and sugar together until pale and fluffy, then add the eggs gradually, beating thoroughly after each addition. Stir in the orange rind and poppy seeds. Sift in the flour and baking powder, then fold in evenly.

3. Add the milk and orange juice, stirring to mix evenly. Spoon the batter into the prepared pan and bake in the preheated oven for 45–50 minutes, or until firm and golden brown. Cool in the pan for 10 minutes, then turn out onto a wire rack to cool.

4. For the syrup, place the sugar and orange juice in a saucepan and heat gently until the sugar melts. Bring to a boil and simmer for about 5 minutes, until reduced and syrupy. Spoon the syrup over the cake while it is still warm. Top with the strips of orange zest and serve warm or cold.

HELPFUL HINT

Be extra careful when turning the cake out onto the wire rack. If the cake sticks a little, then gently ease it away from the pan with the tip of a spatula.

Cinnamon Swirl Cake

SERVES 12

◆ Cooking time:
45–50 minutes

INGREDIENTS
✺ ¾ cup pecans
✺ 2 tsp ground cinnamon
✺ ¼ cup light brown sugar
✺ 2 cups self-rising flour
✺ 1 tsp baking powder
✺ ¾ cup butter, softened, plus extra for greasing
✺ heaping ¾ cup superfine sugar
✺ 3 extra large eggs, beaten
✺ 4 tbsp sour cream

GLAZED PECANS
✺ 1 tbsp light corn syrup
✺ 2 tsp granulated sugar
✺ 12 pecan halves

FROSTING
✺ ¾ cup soft cheese
✺ 1 tbsp maple syrup
✺ 1 cup confectioners' sugar, sifted

Rippled with layers of cinnamon, brown sugar, and ground pecans and topped with a tangy soft cheese frosting, this cake looks and tastes fantastic.

1. Preheat the oven to 350°F/180°C. Grease and line an 8-inch/20-cm square cake pan.

2. Place the pecans, cinnamon, and light brown sugar in a food processor or blender and process for a few seconds, until finely ground.

3. Sift the flour and baking powder into a large bowl. Add the butter, superfine sugar, eggs, and sour cream and, using an electric handheld mixer, beat for 2–3 minutes, until smooth and creamy.

4. Spoon one-third of the cake batter into the prepared pan. Sprinkle half the pecan mixture over it. Repeat these layers again, then gently spread the remaining cake batter on top. Drag a thin knife through the batter to create a swirled effect. Bake in the preheated oven for 45–50 minutes, or until well risen and firm to the touch. Do not turn the oven off. Cool in the pan for 10 minutes, then turn out onto a wire rack to cool completely.

5. For the glazed pecans, place the syrup and sugar in a small saucepan and heat for 1 minute, then stir in the pecans. Spread the mixture on a greased baking sheet and bake in the preheated oven for 15 minutes. Transfer the nuts to a sheet of parchment paper and let cool completely.

6. For the frosting, place the soft cheese and maple syrup in a bowl and beat together until blended. Beat in the confectioners' sugar until smooth. Swirl the frosting over the top of the cake. Cut into pieces and decorate each piece with a glazed pecan.

HELPFUL HINT
Use a figure-eight motion when swirling the knife through the cake batter.

Orange Cake

SERVES 8

◆ Cooking time:
55–60 minutes

INGREDIENTS
✳ 2 small oranges
✳ ¾ cup butter, softened, plus extra for greasing
✳ ¾ cup superfine sugar
✳ 3 eggs, lightly beaten
✳ 1¼ cups self-rising flour
✳ 3 tbsp ground almonds
✳ 3 tbsp light cream

GLAZE & TOPPING
✳ 6 tbsp orange juice
✳ 2 tbsp superfine sugar
✳ 3 white sugar cubes, crushed

Topped with a sweet orange glaze and crushed sugar cubes, this impressive cake makes a great dessert served warm with a spoonful of Greek-style yogurt or sour cream.

1. Preheat the oven to 350°F/180°C. Grease and line a 7-inch/18-cm round cake pan.

2. Pare the zest from the oranges and chop it finely. In a bowl, cream together the butter, sugar, and orange zest until pale and fluffy.

3. Gradually add the beaten eggs to the batter, beating thoroughly after each addition. Gently fold in the flour, ground almonds, and light cream. Spoon the batter into the prepared pan.

4. Bake in the preheated oven for 55–60 minutes, or until a toothpick inserted into the center comes out clean. Let cool slightly.

5. Meanwhile, make the glaze. Put the orange juice into a small saucepan with the superfine sugar. Bring to a boil over low heat and simmer for 5 minutes.

6. Turn out the cake onto a wire rack. Drizzle the glaze over the cake until it has been absorbed and sprinkle with the crushed sugar cubes. Let cool completely before serving.

HELPFUL HINT
As an alternative to oranges, you could try using clementines or tangerines instead.

Blueberry Crumb Cake

SERVES 10

◆ Cooking time:
1–1¼ hours

INGREDIENTS

✳ ¾ cup butter, softened,
plus extra for greasing
✳ heaping ¾ cup
superfine sugar
✳ 3 extra large eggs,
beaten
✳ 4 tbsp buttermilk
✳ 1¾ cups self-rising
flour
✳ ½ cup ground almonds
✳ 1½ cups blueberries

CRUMB TOPPING

✳ ¾ cup self-rising flour
✳ 4 tbsp butter, chilled
and diced
✳ ¼ cup raw brown sugar
✳ ½ cup chopped mixed
nuts

This is a lovely, moist almond cake full of juicy, plump blueberries and topped with a nutty, crumbly crust. It will keep for 2–3 days in an airtight container and tastes great served warm with whipped cream or yogurt.

1. Preheat the oven to 350°F/180°C. Grease and line a 9-inch/23-cm round springform cake pan.

2. Place the butter and superfine sugar in a large bowl and beat together until pale and fluffy, then gradually beat in the eggs. Stir in the buttermilk. Sift over the flour and fold in gently until thoroughly incorporated. Fold in the ground almonds.

3. Spread half of the cake batter into the prepared pan and sprinkle half of the blueberries over it. Spoon the remaining batter over them and spread evenly. Top with the rest of the blueberries.

4. For the crumb topping, sift the flour into a bowl, then add the butter and rub in until the mixture resembles breadcrumbs. Stir in the raw brown sugar and nuts. Sprinkle the mixture evenly over the cake.

5. Bake in the preheated oven for 1–1¼ hours, or until golden brown and firm to the touch. Let cool in the pan for 20 minutes, then unclip the pan and transfer to a wire rack to cool completely. Slice to serve.

HELPFUL HINT
For a variation, replace the blueberries with raspberries, blackberries, or diced peaches.

Spiced Apple & Raisin Cake

SERVES 8–10

◆ Cooking time:
1–1¼ hours

INGREDIENTS

✳ 1 cup unsalted butter, softened, plus extra for greasing

✳ heaping 1 cup light brown sugar

✳ 4 extra large eggs, lightly beaten

✳ scant 1⅔ cups self-rising flour

✳ 2 tsp ground cinnamon

✳ ½ tsp ground nutmeg

✳ ½ cup raisins

✳ 3 small baking apples, peeled, cored, and thinly sliced

✳ 2 tbsp honey, warmed

A lightly spiced cake full of raisins and apples with a sweet honey glaze, this cake will stay moist and delicious for up to a week.

1. Preheat the oven to 350°F/180°C. Grease and line a 9-inch/23-cm round springform cake pan.

2. Place the butter and sugar in a large bowl and beat together until light and fluffy. Gradually beat in the eggs. Sift the flour, cinnamon, and nutmeg into the batter and fold in gently, using a metal spoon. Fold in the raisins.

3. Spoon half of the batter into the prepared pan and smooth the surface. Scatter on half of the sliced apples. Spoon on the rest of the cake batter and gently smooth the surface. Arrange the rest of the apple slices over the top.

4. Bake in the preheated oven for 1–1¼ hours, or until risen, golden brown, and firm to the touch. Let cool in the pan for 10 minutes, then turn out onto a cooling rack. Brush the top with the warmed honey and let cool completely.

HELPFUL HINT

Instead of the honey glaze, drizzle a little maple syrup over the top of the warm cake.

Honey & Almond Cake

SERVES 8

◆ Cooking time:
50 minutes

INGREDIENTS

✳ ⅓ cup soft margarine,
plus extra for greasing

✳ ¼ cup brown sugar

✳ 2 eggs

✳ 1¼ cups self-rising
flour

✳ 1 tsp baking powder

✳ 4 tbsp milk

✳ 2 tbsp honey

✳ ½ cup slivered almonds

SYRUP

✳ ⅔ cup honey

✳ 2 tbsp lemon juice

This light yellow cake has a crunchy almond topping and, after baking, is drenched in a sweet honey and lemon syrup, giving it a deliciously moist and crumbly texture.

1. Preheat the oven to 350°F/180°C. Grease and line a 7-inch/18-cm round cake pan.

2. Place the margarine, brown sugar, eggs, flour, baking powder, milk, and honey in a large mixing bowl and beat well with a wooden spoon for about 1 minute, until all of the ingredients are thoroughly combined.

3. Spoon the batter into the prepared pan, smooth the surface with the back of a spoon or a knife, and sprinkle with half of the almonds. Bake in the preheated oven for about 50 minutes, or until the cake is well risen and a toothpick inserted into the center of the cake comes out clean.

4. Meanwhile, make the syrup. Combine the honey and lemon juice in a small saucepan and simmer over low heat for about 5 minutes, or until the syrup starts to coat the back of a spoon.

5. As soon as the cake comes out of the oven, pour the syrup over it, letting it seep into the middle of the cake, then decorate with the remaining slivered almonds. Let the cake cool for at least 2 hours before slicing.

HELPFUL HINT
Choose a well-flavored honey,
such as orange blossom,
to make this cake taste extra special.

Fruit & Nut Loaf

SERVES 8–10

◆ Cooking time:
1–1¼ hours

INGREDIENTS

✹ ¾ cup butter, softened, plus extra for greasing
✹ heaping ½ cup dark brown sugar
✹ 2 tbsp honey
✹ 3 eggs, beaten
✹ 1¾ cups whole wheat flour
✹ 2¼ tsp baking powder
✹ ½ tsp salt
✹ scant 1 cup raisins
✹ ⅓ cup chopped plumped dried apricots
✹ ⅓ cup candied cherries, quartered
✹ ¼ cup walnuts, coarsely chopped
✹ ¼ cup macadamia nuts, coarsely chopped

BUTTERCREAM

✹ 6 tbsp unsalted butter, softened
✹ 2 tsp finely grated orange rind
✹ 1 tbsp orange juice
✹ 1½ cups confectioners' sugar

Whole wheat flour, honey, dried fruits, and nuts combine to make this wonderful wholesome fruitcake—just right for a mid-morning pick-me-up!

1. Preheat the oven to 325°F/160°C. Grease and line a 9 x 5 x 3-inch/23 x 13 x 8-cm loaf pan.

2. Place the butter, brown sugar, and honey in a large bowl and beat together until very pale and fluffy. Gradually beat in the eggs.

3. Sift the flour, baking powder, and salt into the mixture, tipping any bran left in the sifter into the bowl. Fold in gently until thoroughly incorporated. Fold in the fruit and nuts.

4. Spoon the batter into the prepared pan and gently smooth the surface. Bake in the preheated oven for 45 minutes, then cover the top loosely with aluminum foil. Bake for another 20–30 minutes, or until golden brown and a toothpick inserted into the center comes out clean. Cool in the pan for 15 minutes, then turn out onto a wire rack to cool completely.

5. For the buttercream, place the butter, orange rind, and orange juice in a bowl and beat together until smooth. Gradually beat in the confectioners' sugar. Spread over the top of the cake. Cut into slices to serve.

HELPFUL HINT
Instead of the buttercream, brush with a little warmed honey to give a sticky glaze.

3

4

5

Coconut & Lime Cake

SERVES 8

◆ Cooking time:
1–1¼ hours

INGREDIENTS

✷ ¾ cup unsalted butter, softened, plus extra for greasing

✷ heaping ¾ cup superfine sugar

✷ 3 eggs, beaten

✷ 1 cup self-rising flour

✷ scant 1 cup dry unsweetened shredded coconut

✷ grated rind and juice of 1 lime

ICING

✷ 1½ cups confectioners' sugar

✷ grated rind and juice of 1 lime

✷ ¼ cup dry unsweetened shredded coconut, lightly toasted

This quick and easy-to-bake cake has a wonderful tropical-flavored twist. It has a sweet and buttery, coconut yellow cake that is complemented perfectly by a tangy lime icing.

1. Preheat the oven to 325ºF/160ºC. Grease and line an 8-inch/20-cm round cake pan.

2. Place the butter and superfine sugar in a large bowl and beat together until pale and fluffy. Gradually beat in the eggs. Sift in the flour and gently fold in using a metal spoon. Fold in the coconut and the lime rind and juice.

3. Spoon the batter into the prepared pan and smooth the surface. Bake in the preheated oven for 1–1¼ hours, or until risen, golden, and firm to the touch. Let cool in the pan for 5 minutes, then turn out to cool completely on a wire rack.

4. For the icing, sift the confectioners' sugar into a bowl. Stir in the lime rind and juice to make a smooth icing, adding a few drops of water, if necessary. Spoon the icing over the top of the cake, letting it drizzle down the sides of the cake. Scatter the toasted shredded coconut over the icing and let set.

HELPFUL HINT

To extract the most juice from the limes, roll the fruit firmly over a hard surface before halving and squeezing.

Lemon Cornmeal Cake

SERVES 8

◆ Cooking time:
30–35 minutes

INGREDIENTS

✳ scant 1 cup unsalted butter, plus extra for greasing
✳ 1 cup superfine sugar
✳ finely grated rind and juice of 1 large lemon
✳ 3 eggs, beaten
✳ 1¼ cups ground almonds
✳ scant ¾ cup instant or precooked cornmeal or polenta
✳ 1 tsp baking powder
✳ crème fraîche or lightly whipped heavy cream, to serve

SYRUP

✳ juice of 2 lemons
✳ ¼ cup superfine sugar
✳ 2 tbsp water

This cake contains a golden yellow cornmeal, or more traditionally polenta, which is used in place of flour in this Italian classic. The result is a wonderfully soft cake with a slightly crunchy texture.

1. Preheat the oven to 350°F/180°C. Grease and line an 8-inch/20-cm round deep cake pan.

2. Beat the butter and sugar together until pale and fluffy. Beat in the lemon rind, lemon juice, eggs, and ground almonds. Sift in the cornmeal and baking powder and stir until evenly mixed.

3. Spoon the batter into the prepared pan and smooth the surface. Bake in the preheated oven for 30–35 minutes, or until just firm to the touch and golden brown. Remove the cake from the oven and let cool in the pan for 20 minutes.

4. To make the syrup, place the lemon juice, sugar, and water in a small saucepan. Heat gently, stirring until the sugar has dissolved, then bring to a boil and simmer for 3–4 minutes, or until slightly reduced and syrupy. Turn out the cake onto a wire rack, then brush half of the syrup evenly over the surface. Let cool completely.

5. Cut the cake into slices, drizzle the extra syrup over the top, and serve with crème fraîche or whipped cream.

HELPFUL HINT

This cake is best eaten warm on the day of making. It makes a wonderful dessert when served with crème fraîche or heavy cream.

CHOCOLATE CAKES

3

Chocolate & Vanilla Cake

SERVES 12

♦ Cooking time:
40–50 minutes

INGREDIENTS

✳ oil or melted butter,
for greasing

✳ 1½ cups all-purpose
flour

✳ 1 tbsp baking powder

✳ ¾ cup unsalted butter,
softened

✳ heaping ¾ cup
superfine sugar

✳ 3 eggs, beaten

✳ 2 tbsp unsweetened
cocoa

✳ 2 tbsp milk

✳ 1 tsp vanilla extract

✳ confectioners' sugar,
for dusting

A marbled cake with swirls of contrasting
colors always looks impressive, but when
it is made in a tube-shape pan, it looks
even better!

1. Preheat the oven to 325°F/160°C. Grease a
6¾-cup tube cake pan.

2. Sift the flour and baking powder into a large
bowl and add the butter, superfine sugar, and
eggs. Beat well until the mixture is smooth.
Transfer half of the batter to a separate bowl.
Combine the cocoa and milk and stir into one
bowl of batter. Add the vanilla extract to the
other bowl and mix evenly.

3. Spoon alternate tablespoons of the
two batters into the prepared pan and swirl
lightly with a spatula for a marbled effect.

4. Bake in the preheated oven for 40–50 minutes,
or until risen, firm, and golden brown. Let cool in
the pan for 10 minutes, then turn out and finish
cooling on a wire rack. Dust with confectioners'
sugar before serving.

HELPFUL HINT
Be careful not to overswirl the
batter because you will lose the
marbled effect.

Devil's Food Cake

SERVES 8–10

◆ Cooking time:
35–40 minutes

INGREDIENTS

✳ 5 oz/140 g semisweet chocolate

✳ scant ½ cup milk

✳ 2 tbsp unsweetened cocoa

✳ ½ cup plus 2 tbsp butter, plus extra for greasing

✳ ⅔ cup light brown sugar

✳ 3 eggs, separated

✳ 4 tbsp sour cream

✳ 1¾ cups all-purpose flour

✳ 1 tsp baking soda

FROSTING

✳ 5 oz/140 g semisweet chocolate

✳ ⅓ cup unsweetened cocoa

✳ 4 tbsp sour cream

✳ 1 tbsp light corn syrup

✳ 3 tbsp butter

✳ 4 tbsp water

✳ 1¾ cups confectioners' sugar

This classic cake is a moist and dark chocolate cake smothered in a rich and creamy chocolate frosting. It is a great cake to serve for a birthday celebration because it can be made in advance and is easy to slice!

1. Preheat the oven to 325°F/160°C. Grease and line two 8-inch/20-cm round layer cake pans.

2. Break up the chocolate and place with the milk and cocoa in a heatproof bowl set over a saucepan of gently simmering water, stirring until melted and smooth. Remove from the heat. In a large bowl, beat together the butter and brown sugar until pale and fluffy.

3. Beat in the egg yolks, then the sour cream and melted chocolate mixture. Sift in the flour and baking soda, then fold in evenly. In a separate bowl, whip the egg whites until stiff enough to hold firm peaks. Fold into the mixture lightly and evenly.

4. Divide the batter between the prepared cake pans, smooth the surfaces, and bake in the preheated oven for 35–40 minutes, or until risen and firm to the touch. Cool in the pans for 10 minutes, then turn out onto a wire rack.

5. For the frosting, place the chocolate, cocoa, sour cream, corn syrup, butter, and water in a saucepan and heat gently without boiling, until melted. Remove from the heat and add the confectioners' sugar, stirring until smooth. Cool, stirring occasionally, until the mixture begins to thicken and hold its shape.

6. Split the cakes in half horizontally with a sharp knife to make four layers. Sandwich the cakes together with about one-third of the frosting. Spread the remainder over the top and sides of the cakes, swirling with a spatula.

HELPFUL HINT
Use a good-quality chocolate for the best flavor—one with at least 50% cocoa.

Mocha Cake

SERVES 10–12

◆ Cooking time:
25–30 minutes

INGREDIENTS

✸ 2 cups self-rising flour
✸ 1 tsp baking powder
✸ 2 tbsp unsweetened cocoa powder
✸ 1 cup butter, softened, plus extra for greasing
✸ heaping 1 cup light brown sugar
✸ 4 extra large eggs, beaten
✸ 4 oz/115 g semisweet chocolate, melted
✸ 2 tbsp superfine sugar
✸ 3 tbsp strong black coffee

FROSTING

✸ 6 tbsp unsalted butter, softened
✸ generous 1 cup mascarpone cheese
✸ ½ cup confectioners' sugar
✸ 2 tbsp strong black coffee
✸ unsweetened cocoa powder, for dusting
✸ chocolate-coated coffee beans, to decorate

This delicious cake is the perfect combination of two classic flavors—chocolate and coffee.

1. Preheat the oven to 350°F/180°C. Grease and line two 8-inch/20-cm round layer cake pans.

2. Sift the flour, baking powder, and cocoa into a large bowl. Add the butter, light brown sugar, and eggs and, using an electric handheld mixer, beat together for 3–4 minutes, until the mixture is very smooth and creamy. Fold in the melted chocolate.

3. Divide the batter between the prepared cake pans and bake in the preheated oven for 25–30 minutes, or until risen and firm to the touch.

4. Place the superfine sugar and black coffee in a small saucepan and heat gently for 1–2 minutes. Cool for 10 minutes. Pierce the tops of the warm cakes all over with a toothpick and spoon the coffee syrup over the cakes. Let the cakes cool in the pans.

5. For the frosting, place the butter and mascarpone in a bowl and beat together until well blended. Beat in the confectioners' sugar and coffee until smooth.

6. Remove the cakes from the pans and sandwich together with half of the frosting. Swirl the remaining frosting over the top of the cake. Dust with unsweetened cocoa powder and decorate with chocolate-coated coffee beans. Cut into slices to serve.

HELPFUL HINT
Add a splash of coffee-flavored liqueur to the warm syrup before spooning it over the cakes.

2

3

6

Chocolate Layer Cake

SERVES 8

◆ Cooking time:
25–30 minutes

INGREDIENTS

✳ oil or melted butter,
for greasing

✳ 1⅓ cups all-purpose
flour

✳ 2 tbsp unsweetened
cocoa

✳ 1 tbsp baking powder

✳ ¾ cup unsalted butter,
softened

✳ heaping ¾ cup
superfine sugar

✳ 3 eggs, beaten

✳ 1 tsp vanilla extract

✳ 2 tbsp milk

✳ ⅔ cup chocolate-
hazelnut spread

✳ confectioners' sugar,
for dusting

This chocolate variation on a classic yellow layer cake is quick and easy to make and will be a definite favorite with children and chocolate lovers.

1. Preheat the oven to 350°F/180°C. Grease and line two 8-inch/20-cm round layer cake pans.

2. Sift the flour, cocoa, and baking powder into a large bowl and add the butter, superfine sugar, eggs, and vanilla extract. Beat well until the batter is smooth, then stir in the milk.

3. Divide the batter between the prepared pans and smooth the surfaces with a spatula. Bake in the preheated oven for 25–30 minutes, or until golden brown and firm to the touch. Let cool in the pans for 2–3 minutes, then turn out to cool on a wire rack.

4. When the cakes have cooled completely, sandwich them together with the chocolate-hazelnut spread, then dust with confectioners' sugar and serve.

HELPFUL HINT

Instead of the chocolate-hazelnut spread filling, try mint-flavored buttercream (see page 88).

Chocolate Heart Cake

SERVES 10

✦ Cooking time:
45–55 minutes

INGREDIENTS
✹ 1½ cups all-purpose flour
✹ 1 tbsp baking powder
✹ ¾ cup unsalted butter, softened, plus extra for greasing
✹ heaping ¾ cup superfine sugar
✹ 3 eggs, beaten
✹ 1 tsp vanilla extract
✹ ¼ cup grated white chocolate
✹ 2 tbsp white rum (optional)
✹ candied violets, to decorate

FROSTING
✹ 7 oz/200 g white chocolate, broken into pieces
✹ 2 tbsp milk
✹ scant 1 cup heavy cream

A wonderful cake to serve for a special occasion, this heart shape cake is a white chocolate- and rum-flavored cake with a rich and creamy white chocolate frosting. Bake the cake a day in advance and frost and decorate a few hours before serving.

1. Preheat the oven to 325°F/160°C. Grease a 6¾-cup heart shape cake pan.

2. Sift the flour and baking powder into a bowl and add the butter, sugar, eggs, and vanilla extract. Beat well until smooth, then stir in the grated chocolate.

3. Spoon the batter into the prepared pan and smooth the surface. Bake in the preheated oven for 45–55 minutes, or until risen, firm, and golden brown. Let cool in the pan for 10 minutes, then turn out onto a wire rack to finish cooling.

4. To make the frosting, melt the chocolate with the milk in a heatproof bowl set over a pan of gently simmering water. Remove from the heat and stir until smooth, then let cool for 10 minutes. Whip the cream until it holds soft peaks, then fold into the cooled chocolate mixture.

5. Sprinkle the cake with the rum, if using. Spread the frosting over the top and sides of the cake, swirling with a spatula, then decorate with candied violets.

HELPFUL HINT
Chill the chocolate in the refrigerator for 30 minutes before grating to stop it from melting too quickly.

Chocolate Chip Cake

SERVES 9

◆ Cooking time:
40–45 minutes

INGREDIENTS

❋ 2 cups self-rising flour
❋ ½ tsp baking powder
❋ 1 cup butter, softened, plus extra for greasing
❋ heaping 1 cup superfine sugar
❋ ½ cup ground almonds
❋ 4 eggs
❋ 1 tsp vanilla extract
❋ scant 1 cup milk chocolate chips
❋ 2 oz/55 g milk or semisweet chocolate, melted, to decorate
❋ 2 oz/55 g white chocolate, melted, to decorate

This yellow cake is made by the quick all-in-one method. This is where all the ingredients are beaten together until smooth and creamy.

1. Preheat the oven to 350°F/180°C. Grease and line a 9-inch/23-cm square shallow cake pan.

2. Sift the flour and baking powder into a large bowl. Add the butter, sugar, ground almonds, eggs, and vanilla extract. Using an electric handheld mixer, beat until the batter is very smooth and creamy. Fold in half of the chocolate chips.

3. Spoon the cake batter into the prepared pan and gently smooth the surface. Sprinkle the rest of the chocolate chips over it. Bake in the preheated oven for 40–45 minutes, or until well risen, golden, and springy to the touch.

4. Let the cake cool in the pan for 5 minutes, then turn out onto a wire rack to cool completely.

5. To decorate, spoon the melted chocolates into two separate paper pastry bags. Snip off the ends and drizzle the chocolates in squiggly lines over the cake. Let set. Cut into squares and serve.

HELPFUL HINT

Freeze individual squares in aluminum foil—they are perfect for lunch bags or picnics.

2

3

5

Red Velvet Cake

SERVES 12

✦ Cooking time:
25–30 minutes

INGREDIENTS

✱ 1 cup unsalted butter, plus extra for greasing
✱ 4 tbsp water
✱ ½ cup unsweetened cocoa
✱ 3 eggs
✱ generous 1 cup buttermilk
✱ 2 tsp vanilla extract
✱ 2 tbsp red edible food coloring
✱ 2½ cups all-purpose flour
✱ ½ cup cornstarch
✱ 1½ tsp baking powder
✱ scant 1½ cups superfine sugar

FROSTING

✱ generous 1 cup cream cheese
✱ 3 tbsp unsalted butter
✱ 3 tbsp superfine sugar
✱ 1 tsp vanilla extract

This popular American favorite is a rich buttermilk-flavor chocolate cake, colored deep red with edible food coloring and topped with a traditional vanilla cream cheese frosting.

1. Preheat the oven to 375°F/190°C. Grease and line two 9-inch/23-cm round layer cake pans.

2. Place the butter, water, and cocoa in a small saucepan and heat gently, without boiling, stirring until melted and smooth. Remove from the heat and let cool slightly.

3. Beat together the eggs, buttermilk, vanilla extract, and food coloring until frothy. Beat in the butter mixture. Sift together the flour, cornstarch, and baking powder, then stir quickly and evenly into the batter with the superfine sugar.

4. Spoon the batter into the prepared pans and bake in the preheated oven for 25–30 minutes, or until risen and firm to the touch. Cool in the pans for 3–4 minutes, then turn out onto a wire rack to cool completely.

5. To make the frosting, beat together all the ingredients until smooth. Use about half of the frosting to sandwich the cakes together, then spread the remainder over the top, swirling with a metal spatula.

HELPFUL HINT

Take care not to overbeat the cream cheese frosting as it can go a little runny. If this happens, chill in the refrigerator for 1 hour.

Chocolate Coconut Cake

SERVES 6

◆ Cooking time:
40 minutes

INGREDIENTS

✳ ¾ cup butter or
margarine, plus extra for
greasing
✳ ¾ cup superfine sugar
✳ 3 eggs, beaten
✳ 1¼ cups self-rising
flour
✳ 2 tbsp unsweetened
cocoa

FROSTING

✳ 1¾ oz/50 g semisweet
chocolate, broken into
pieces
✳ 5 tbsp milk
✳ 1 tsp butter
✳ ¾ cup confectioners'
sugar
✳ ½ cup dry unsweetened
flaked coconut
✳ ⅔ cup heavy cream,
whipped

**This sumptuous chocolate cream cake
is a variation on the traditional Australian
lamington cake—small yellow cake squares
covered in chocolate frosting and dry
unsweetened coconut.**

1. Preheat the oven to 350°F/180°C. Grease and
line a 9-inch/23-cm loaf pan.

2. Beat together the butter or margarine and
superfine sugar in a bowl until light and fluffy.
Gradually add the eggs, beating well after each
addition. Sift the flour and cocoa together. Fold
into the batter.

3. Spoon the batter into the prepared pan and
smooth the surface. Bake in the preheated oven
for 40 minutes, or until springy to the touch. Let
cool for 4 minutes in the pan, then turn out
onto a wire rack to cool completely.

4. For the frosting, place the chocolate, milk,
and butter in a heatproof bowl set over a pan of
gently simmering water. Stir until the chocolate
has melted. Add the confectioners' sugar and
beat until smooth. Let the frosting cool until it is
thick enough to spread, then spread it all over
the cake. Sprinkle with the dry unsweetened
coconut and let stand until the frosting has set.

5. Cut a V-shape wedge from the top of the
cake. Put the cream in a pastry bag fitted with a
plain or star tip. Pipe the cream down the center
of the channel and replace the wedge of cake on
top of the cream. Pipe cream down either side of
the wedge of cake. Serve.

HELPFUL HINT
Lightly toast the coconut in a hot
oven for just a few minutes before
using to produce a nuttier flavor.

Chocolate & Sour Cherry Cake

SERVES 12

◆ Cooking time:
40–45 minutes

INGREDIENTS

✳ 6 oz/175 g semisweet chocolate, broken into pieces
✳ ½ cup butter, diced, plus extra for greasing
✳ 3 extra large eggs, separated
✳ heaping ½ cup dark brown sugar
✳ 1 cup self-rising flour, sifted
✳ ½ cup ground almonds
✳ ¾ cup dried cherries, chopped
✳ chocolate curls, unsweetened cocoa, and fresh cherries, to decorate

FROSTING

✳ 6 oz/175 g semisweet chocolate, broken into pieces
✳ 5 tbsp heavy cream
✳ 4 tbsp unsalted butter
✳ 1 tbsp rum

An intensely dark and rich chocolate cake with a rum-flavored chocolate frosting—this is definitely one for the adults. Serve with a spoon of sour cream for a delicious dessert.

1. Preheat the oven to 350°F/180°C. Grease and line an 8-inch/20-cm round cake pan.

2. Place the chocolate and butter in a large heatproof bowl set over a saucepan of simmering water until melted. Remove from the heat and stir until smooth. Cool for 10 minutes, stirring occasionally.

3. Place the egg yolks and sugar in a large bowl and, using an electric handheld mixer, beat until pale and creamy. Add the melted chocolate and beat until thoroughly combined. Fold in the flour, ground almonds, and dried cherries.

4. In a separate bowl, whisk the egg whites until soft peaks form, then gently fold into the chocolate mixture. Spoon the batter into the prepared pan and gently smooth the surface.

5. Bake in the preheated oven for 40–45 minutes, or until just firm to the touch and a toothpick inserted into the center comes out clean. Cool in the pan for 10 minutes, then turn out onto a wire rack to cool completely.

6. For the frosting, place the chocolate, cream, and butter in a heatproof bowl set over a saucepan of simmering water until melted, then remove from the heat, and beat in the rum. Cool for 20 minutes, then chill in the refrigerator, stirring occasionally, for about 30 minutes, or until thick enough to spread.

7. Spread the frosting over the top of the cake. Decorate with chocolate curls and dust lightly with unsweetened cocoa. Top with the fresh cherries.

HELPFUL HINT
For extra flavor, pierce the warm cake with a toothpick and spoon a little cherry liqueur over it.

Chocolate Ganache

SERVES 10

✦ Cooking time:
40 minutes

INGREDIENTS

✳ ¾ cup unsalted butter,
plus extra for greasing

✳ ¾ cup superfine sugar

✳ 4 eggs, lightly beaten

✳ 1¾ cups self-rising
flour

✳ 1 tbsp unsweetened
cocoa

✳ 1¾ oz/50 g semisweet
chocolate, melted

✳ 7 oz/200 g chocolate-
flavored confectionery
coating, to decorate

GANACHE

✳ 2 cups heavy cream

✳ 13 oz/375 g semisweet
chocolate, broken into
pieces

This impressive looking cake is a rich chocolate cake decorated with a divinely glossy chocolate ganache. It takes a little time and skill to make, but the effort will be well worth it.

1. Preheat the oven to 350°F/180°C. Grease and line an 8-inch/20-cm round springform cake pan.

2. Beat the butter and sugar together in a bowl until light and fluffy. Gradually add the eggs, beating well after each addition. Sift the flour and cocoa together, then fold into the cake batter. Fold in the melted chocolate.

3. Pour into the prepared pan and smooth the surface. Bake in the preheated oven for 40 minutes, or until springy to the touch. Let the cake cool for 5 minutes in the pan, then turn out onto a wire rack and let cool completely. Cut the cooled cake into two layers.

4. To make the ganache, place the cream in a saucepan and bring to a boil, stirring. Add the chocolate and stir until melted. Pour into a bowl, let cool, then chill for 2 hours, or until set and firm. Whisk the mixture until light and fluffy and set aside.

5. Reserve one-third of the ganache. Use the remainder to sandwich the cake together and spread over the cake.

6. Melt the confectionery coating and spread it over a large sheet of parchment paper. Let cool until just set. Cut into strips a little wider than the height of the cake. Place the strips around the edge of the cake, overlapping them slightly.

7. Pipe the reserved ganache in teardrops or shells to cover the top of the cake. Let chill for 1 hour before serving.

HELPFUL HINT
For a simpler decoration, spread the ganache smoothly over the top of the cake, using a large palette knife, and decorate with chocolate shavings.

SOMETHING SPECIAL

4

Chocolate Brownie Cake

SERVES 10

◆ Cooking time:
25–30 minutes

INGREDIENTS

✳ scant 1 cup butter, plus
extra for greasing
✳ 4 oz/115 g semisweet
chocolate, broken into
pieces
✳ 1¼ cups granulated
sugar
✳ ½ cup light brown
sugar
✳ 4 eggs, beaten
✳ ¾ cup all-purpose flour
✳ 1 tsp vanilla extract
✳ pinch of salt
✳ ½ cup dried cranberries
✳ scant ½ cup toasted
slivered almonds,
plus extra to decorate

FROSTING

✳ 4 oz/115 g semisweet
chocolate, broken into
pieces
✳ 2 tbsp butter
✳ 2 cups confectioners'
sugar
✳ 3–4 tbsp milk

All the family will love this sweet, fudgy chocolate cake. It is delicious served with a mug of hot chocolate or a creamy vanilla milkshake. Alternatively, serve warm with ice cream for a wickedly indulgent dessert.

1. Preheat the oven to 350°F/180°C. Grease and line two 7-inch/18-cm round layer cake pans.

2. Place the butter in a heavy-bottom pan and add the chocolate. Heat gently, stirring frequently, until the mixture has melted. Remove from the heat and stir until smooth. Add the sugars, stir well, then let cool for 10 minutes.

3. Gradually add the eggs to the cooled chocolate mixture, beating well after each addition. Stir in the flour, vanilla extract, and salt. Stir in the cranberries and slivered almonds, mix, then divide between the prepared cake pans.

4. Bake in the preheated oven for 25–30 minutes, or until springy to the touch. Remove from the oven and let cool slightly in the pan before turning out onto a wire rack to cool completely.

5. To make the frosting, melt the chocolate and butter in a heavy-bottom pan and stir until smooth. Gradually beat in the confectioners' sugar with enough milk to create a smooth spreading consistency. Use a little of the frosting to sandwich the two cakes together, then spread the top and sides with the remainder, swirling the top to create a decorative effect. Sprinkle with slivered almonds and let the frosting set before serving.

HELPFUL HINT
Be careful not to overcook the cakes—they should still be a little soft in the middle, just like classic brownies.

Hummingbird Cake

SERVES 10

◆ Cooking time:
25–30 minutes

INGREDIENTS

✳ 2¼ cups all-purpose flour
✳ 1¼ cups superfine sugar
✳ 1 tsp ground cinnamon
✳ 1 tsp baking soda
✳ 3 eggs, beaten
✳ scant 1 cup sunflower oil, plus extra for greasing
✳ scant 1 cup pecans, coarsely chopped, plus extra to decorate
✳ 1 cup mashed ripe bananas (about 3 bananas)
✳ 2¼ cups drained, crushed canned pineapple, plus 4 tbsp juice from the can

FROSTING

✳ ¾ cup cream cheese
✳ ¼ cup unsalted butter
✳ 1 tsp vanilla extract
✳ 3½ cups confectioners' sugar

Originating from the South, this fruity layer cake is made with crushed pineapple, pecans, and ripe bananas and has a sweet and creamy vanilla frosting.

1. Preheat the oven to 350°F/180°C. Grease and line three 9-inch/23-cm round layer cake pans.

2. Sift the flour, superfine sugar, cinnamon, and baking soda into a large bowl. Add the eggs, oil, pecans, bananas, and pineapple with the juice and stir with a wooden spoon until evenly mixed.

3. Divide the batter among the prepared pans, spreading it evenly. Bake in the preheated oven for 25–30 minutes, or until golden brown and firm to the touch.

4. Remove the cakes from the oven and let cool for 10 minutes in the pans before turning out onto wire racks to cool.

5. For the frosting, beat together the cream cheese, butter, and vanilla extract in a bowl until smooth. Sift in the confectioners' sugar and mix until smooth.

6. Sandwich the cakes together with half of the frosting, spread the remaining frosting over the top, then sprinkle with pecans to decorate.

HELPFUL HINT
The baked cakes are fragile, so be extra careful when turning them out onto wire racks.

Boston Cream Pie

SERVES 10

◆ Cooking time:
20–25 minutes

INGREDIENTS
✳ 4 extra large eggs
✳ heaping ½ cup superfine sugar
✳ 1 cup all-purpose flour
✳ 3 tbsp butter, melted and cooled, plus extra for greasing

PASTRY CREAM
✳ 2 eggs
✳ ¼ cup superfine sugar
✳ 1 tsp vanilla extract
✳ 2 tbsp all-purpose flour
✳ 2 tbsp cornstarch
✳ 1¼ cups milk
✳ ⅔ cup heavy cream, softly whipped

CHOCOLATE GLAZE
✳ 4 oz/115 g semisweet chocolate, grated
✳ 1 tbsp light corn syrup
✳ 2 tbsp unsalted butter
✳ ⅔ cup heavy cream

Not a pie at all but an indulgent combination of two light cakes, sandwiched with a rich vanilla pastry cream and topped with a glossy chocolate glaze.

1. Preheat the oven to 350°F/180°C. Grease and line two 9-inch/23-cm round layer cake pans.

2. Place the eggs and sugar in a heatproof bowl set over a saucepan of simmering water. Using an electric handheld mixer, beat together until the mixture is thick and pale and leaves a trail on the surface when the beaters are lifted.

3. Sift in the flour and fold in gently. Pour the butter in a thin stream over the mixture and fold in until just incorporated. Divide the cake batter between the prepared pans and bake in the preheated oven for 20–25 minutes, or until light golden and springy to the touch. Cool in the pans for 5 minutes, then turn out onto a wire rack to cool completely.

4. For the pastry cream, whisk together the eggs, sugar, and vanilla extract. Blend the flour and cornstarch to a paste with 4 tablespoons of the milk, then whisk into the egg mixture. Heat the remaining milk until almost boiling and pour onto the egg mixture, stirring continuously. Return to the pan and cook over low heat, whisking continuously, until smooth and thickened. Pour into a bowl and cover with dampened wax paper. Let stand until cold, then fold in the whipped cream.

5. For the glaze, place the chocolate, light corn syrup, and butter in a heatproof bowl. Heat the cream until it is almost boiling, then pour it over the chocolate. Let stand for 1 minute, then stir until smooth.

6. To assemble, sandwich the cakes together with the pastry cream. Spread the chocolate glaze over the top of the cake. Cut into slices to serve.

HELPFUL HINT
Be careful not to overmix when folding in the flour and melted butter or the cake will have a heavy texture.

Sticky Ginger Loaf

SERVES 8–10

◆ Cooking time:
1–1¼ hours

INGREDIENTS

✳ oil or melted butter, for greasing
✳ 1½ cups all-purpose flour
✳ 1 tbsp baking powder
✳ 1 tbsp ground ginger
✳ ¾ cup sunflower oil
✳ scant ½ cup dark brown sugar
✳ ⅓ cup light corn syrup
✳ 3 eggs, beaten
✳ 3 pieces preserved ginger in syrup, drained and finely chopped, plus 2 tbsp syrup from the jar
✳ sliced preserved ginger, to decorate

This is a great cake for novice bakers to make because it is so easy—simply mix all the ingredients to a smooth batter, pour into the pan, and bake.

1. Preheat the oven to 350°F/180°C. Grease and line a 9 x 5 x 3-inch/23 x 13 x 8-cm loaf pan.

2. Sift the flour, baking powder, and ground ginger into a large bowl. Add the oil, sugar, corn syrup, and eggs, then beat well to a smooth batter. Stir in the chopped ginger.

3. Pour the batter into the prepared pan. Bake in the preheated oven for 1–1¼ hours, or until well risen and firm.

4. Let cool in the pan for 10 minutes, then turn out to finish cooling on a wire rack. To serve, brush the cake with the ginger syrup, arrange the sliced ginger on top, and cut into slices.

HELPFUL HINT

Let the corn syrup stand in a warm place for 30 minutes before using to make it easier to pour and measure.

Banana & Pecan Cake

SERVES 6

✦ Cooking time:
25–30 minutes

INGREDIENTS
✳ oil or melted butter,
for greasing
✳ 1½ cups all-purpose
flour
✳ 1 tbsp baking powder
✳ ¾ cup unsalted butter,
softened
✳ heaping ¾ cup
superfine sugar
✳ 3 eggs, beaten
✳ 1 tsp vanilla extract
✳ ⅓ cup finely chopped
pecans
✳ scant ¼ cup dulce de
leche

FILLING AND TOPPING
✳ 2 bananas
✳ 5 tbsp dulce de leche
✳ scant ½ cup heavy
cream
✳ pecan halves,
to decorate

A variation on the classic dessert, this melt-in-your-mouth cake is an irresistible combination of rich caramel, pecans, bananas, and whipped cream!

1. Preheat the oven to 350°F/180°C. Grease and line two 8-inch/20-cm round layer cake pans.

2. Sift the flour and baking powder into a large bowl and add the butter, sugar, eggs, and vanilla extract. Beat well until the batter is smooth, then stir in the chopped pecans. Add the dulce de leche and stir to swirl through the mix.

3. Spoon the batter into the prepared pans and smooth the surfaces with a spatula. Bake in the preheated oven for 25–30 minutes, or until risen, firm, and golden brown. Let cool in the pans for 2–3 minutes, then turn out to finish cooling on a wire rack.

4. Reserve a few slices of banana for decoration and mash the remainder. Mix the mashed bananas with 3 tablespoons of the dulce de leche and use to sandwich the cakes together.

5. Whip the cream until thick, then swirl in the remaining dulce de leche. Spread over the cake and decorate with the reserved banana slices and the pecan halves.

HELPFUL HINT
Brush the banana slices with a little lemon juice to stop them from browning before placing them on the top of the cake.

Squash & Orange Cake

SERVES 10–12

◆ Cooking time:
1 hour

INGREDIENTS

✳ ¾ cup butter, softened,
plus extra for greasing

✳ ¾ cup light brown sugar

✳ 3 eggs, beaten

✳ finely grated rind and
juice of 1 orange

✳ 2 cups whole wheat
flour

✳ 3 tsp baking powder

✳ 1 tsp ground cinnamon

✳ 1⅓ cups coarsely
grated butternut squash

✳ heaping ¾ cup raisins

TOPPING

✳ 1 cup cream cheese

✳ ¼ cup confectioners'
sugar, sifted

✳ 1 tsp finely grated
orange rind (reserved
from cake ingredients)

✳ 2–3 tsp freshly
squeezed orange juice
(reserved from cake
ingredients)

✳ thinly pared orange
zest, to decorate

Grated butternut squash gives this unusual cake a really moist and crumbly texture. Topped with a tangy orange frosting, it is a deliciously wholesome treat that everyone will love!

1. Preheat the oven to 350°F/180°C. Grease and line a 7-inch/18-cm round deep cake pan.

2. Beat the butter and light brown sugar together in a bowl until light and fluffy. Gradually beat in the eggs, beating well after each addition. Reserve 1 teaspoon of the orange rind for the topping, then beat the remaining orange rind into the mixture.

3. Fold in the flour, baking powder, and cinnamon, then fold in the squash, raisins, and a little orange juice, if necessary (about 1 tablespoon) to create a fairly soft consistency. Set aside the remaining orange juice.

4. Spoon the batter into the prepared pan and smooth the surface. Bake in the preheated oven for about 1 hour, or until risen, firm to the touch, and deep golden brown. Remove from the oven and cool in the pan for a few minutes, then turn out onto a wire rack. Remove the lining paper and let cool completely.

5. To make the topping, beat the cream cheese, confectioners' sugar, reserved grated orange rind, and 2–3 teaspoons of the reserved orange juice together in a bowl until smooth and combined. Spread over the top of the cold cake, swirling it attractively, then sprinkle with pared orange zest. Serve immediately in slices.

HELPFUL HINT
Because of its moist texture and cream cheese topping, this cake is best kept in the refrigerator and eaten within two days of making.

Grasshopper Cake

SERVES 8

◆ Cooking time:
1¼ hours

INGREDIENTS

✳ generous 1 cup milk
✳ 1 tbsp lemon juice
✳ 2½ cups self-rising flour
✳ 2 tbsp unsweetened cocoa
✳ 1 tsp baking soda
✳ scant ½ cup butter, softened, plus extra for greasing
✳ heaping 1 cup superfine sugar
✳ 2 extra large eggs
✳ 3½ oz/100 g semisweet chocolate, melted
✳ 1 oz/25 g milk chocolate shavings, to decorate

FROSTING

✳ scant 1 cup unsalted butter, softened
✳ generous 1 cup heavy cream
✳ 3½ cups confectioners' sugar, sifted
✳ 1 tsp peppermint extract
✳ few drops of green food coloring

Named after a crème de menthe cocktail, this decadent gâteau is made up of layers of rich, moist chocolate cake with a creamy mint-flavor buttercream.

1. Preheat the oven to 325°F/160°C. Grease and line an 8-inch/20-cm round deep cake pan.

2. Pour the milk into a pitcher and add the lemon juice. Let stand for 15 minutes—the milk will start to curdle but this is fine.

3. Sift the flour, cocoa, and baking soda into a large bowl. Add the butter, superfine sugar, and eggs and pour in the milk mixture. Beat with an electric handheld mixer until thoroughly combined. Whisk in the melted chocolate.

4. Spoon the batter into the prepared pan and smooth the surface. Bake in the preheated oven for about 1¼ hours, or until the cake is risen and a toothpick inserted into the center comes out clean. Cool in the pan for 20 minutes, then turn out onto a wire rack to cool completely.

5. For the frosting, place the butter in a bowl and beat with an electric handheld mixer for 2–3 minutes, until pale and creamy. Beat in two-thirds of the cream, then gradually beat in the confectioners' sugar. Add the rest of the cream and continue beating for 1–2 minutes, until the buttercream is very light and fluffy. Stir in the peppermint extract and enough food coloring to create a pale green color.

6. Slice the cake horizontally into three equal rounds. Sandwich the rounds together with half of the buttercream. Spread the remaining buttercream over the top and sides of the cake. Decorate with the chocolate shavings. Slice and serve.

HELPFUL HINT

For an alcoholic version, flavor the buttercream with a couple of spoonfuls of crème de menthe instead of the peppermint extract.

White Chocolate Coffee Cake

SERVES 8–10

◆ Cooking time:
25–30 minutes

INGREDIENTS

✳ 3 tbsp unsalted butter, plus extra for greasing
✳ 3 oz/85 g white chocolate, broken into pieces
✳ ⅔ cup superfine sugar
✳ 4 extra large eggs, beaten
✳ 2 tbsp very strong black coffee
✳ 1 tsp vanilla extract
✳ heaping 1 cup all-purpose flour
✳ white chocolate curls, to decorate

FROSTING

✳ 6 oz/175 g white chocolate, broken into pieces
✳ 6 tbsp unsalted butter
✳ generous ½ cup sour cream
✳ heaping 1 cup confectioners' sugar, sifted
✳ 1 tbsp coffee liqueur or very strong black coffee

Coffee and white chocolate go together particularly well in this decadent layer cake. Decorated with elegant chocolate curls, it is ideal to serve as an after-dinner dessert with coffee or liqueurs.

1. Preheat the oven to 350°F/180°C. Grease and line two 8-inch/20-cm round layer cake pans.

2. Place the butter and chocolate in a bowl set over a saucepan of hot, but not simmering, water and heat over very low heat until just melted. Stir to mix lightly, then remove from the heat.

3. Place the superfine sugar, eggs, coffee, and vanilla extract in a large bowl set over a saucepan of hot water and beat hard with an electric handheld mixer until the batter is pale and thick enough to leave a trail when the beaters are lifted.

4. Remove from the heat, sift in the flour, and fold in lightly and evenly. Quickly fold in the butter-and-chocolate mixture, then divide the batter between the prepared pans.

5. Bake in the preheated oven for 25–30 minutes, or until risen, golden brown, and springy to the touch. Cool in the pans for 2 minutes, then run a knife around the edges to loosen and turn out onto a wire rack to cool.

6. For the frosting, place the chocolate and butter in a bowl set over a saucepan of hot water and heat gently until melted. Remove from the heat, stir in the sour cream, then add the confectioners' sugar and coffee liqueur and mix until smooth. Chill the frosting for at least 30 minutes, stirring occasionally, until it becomes thick and glossy.

7. Use about one-third of the frosting to sandwich the cakes together. Spread the remainder over the top and sides, swirling with a spatula. Arrange the chocolate curls over the top of the cake and let set.

HELPFUL HINT

For chocolate curls, spread melted white chocolate onto a clean, flat surface. Let set, then drag a thin blade across the surface at a slight angle.

Blueberry Swirl Cake

SERVES 8–10

◆ Cooking time:
20–25 minutes

INGREDIENTS

✳ oil or melted butter,
for greasing

✳ 1½ cups all-purpose
flour

✳ 1 tbsp baking powder

✳ ¾ cup unsalted butter,
softened

✳ heaping ¾ cup
superfine sugar

✳ 3 eggs, beaten

✳ 1 tsp orange flower
water

✳ 2 tbsp orange juice

FILLING & FROSTING

✳ 1 cup cream cheese

✳ 1 cup confectioners'
sugar, sifted

✳ 2 cups fresh
blueberries

This cake has a lovely fragrant orange flavor and a creamy frosting swirled with fresh blueberry puree. It is delicious served as a simple summer dessert or afternoon treat.

1. Preheat the oven to 325°F/160°C. Grease and line three 8-inch/20-cm round layer cake pans.

2. Sift the flour and baking powder into a large bowl and add the butter, superfine sugar, eggs, and orange flower water. Beat well until the mixture is smooth, then stir in the orange juice.

3. Divide the batter between the prepared pans and smooth the surfaces with a spatula. Bake in the preheated oven for 20–25 minutes, or until risen, firm, and golden brown.

4. Let cool in the pans for 2–3 minutes, then turn out to finish cooling on a wire rack.

5. For the frosting, beat together the cream cheese and confectioners' sugar until smooth. Transfer about two-thirds of the mixture to a separate bowl and stir in 1¼ cups of the blueberries, then use this to sandwich the cakes together.

6. Rub the remaining blueberries through a fine mesh strainer to make a smooth puree. Spread the remaining frosting on top of the cake and swirl the blueberry puree through it.

HELPFUL HINT
Add a splash of orange flower water to the frosting for an extra boost of flavor.

Frosted Raspberry Tube Cake

SERVES 8–10

◆ Cooking time:
40–45 minutes

INGREDIENTS
✳ oil or melted butter,
for greasing
✳ 1½ cups all-purpose
flour
✳ 1 tbsp baking powder
✳ ¾ cup unsalted butter,
softened
✳ heaping ¾ cup
superfine sugar
✳ 3 eggs, beaten
✳ 1 tsp almond extract
✳ ⅔ cup ground almonds
✳ 1⅓ cups fresh
raspberries
✳ toasted slivered
almonds, to decorate

FROSTING
✳ 1 extra large egg white
✳ 1¼ cups confectioners'
sugar
✳ 1 tbsp light corn syrup
✳ ¼ tsp cream of tartar

Cakes made in a tube cake pan always look impressive, and this delicious almond and raspberry cake is no exception. The fresh fruit and frosting topping add a delicious finishing touch and make it a perfect dessert for a dinner party.

1. Preheat the oven to 325°F/160°C. Grease a 6¾-cup tube cake pan.

2. Sift the flour and baking powder into a large bowl and add the butter, superfine sugar, eggs, and almond extract. Beat well until the batter is smooth, then stir in the ground almonds. Mash half of the raspberries with a fork and stir into the batter.

3. Spoon the batter into the prepared pan and smooth the surface with a spatula. Bake in the preheated oven for 40–45 minutes, or until risen, firm, and golden brown.

4. Let cool in the pan for 10 minutes, then turn out carefully onto a wire rack to finish cooling.

5. For the frosting, place the egg white, confectioners' sugar, corn syrup, and cream of tartar in a bowl over a saucepan of hot water and whisk vigorously with an electric handheld mixer until thick enough to hold its shape.

6. Quickly swirl the frosting over the cake. Decorate with the remaining raspberries and the slivered almonds.

HELPFUL HINT
If you are using a cake pan that does not have a nonstick coating, place parchment paper in the greased pan.